The Provocateur

Spilling beans by all means

BALVINDER RUBY

About the Author

Balvinder Ruby is an entrepreneur, provocateur, thought leader, author, and social activist. Open-minded and receptive to fresh ideas, he also has a deep appreciation for aesthetics and beauty. A prolific writer, Ruby has recently authored the following four books:

- The Provocateur: Spilling Beans by All Means
- New World Order: Rise of the Transnational Corporate Republic
- Climate Conundrum: The Agendas and Forces at Play
- Fractured Mirrors: Power, Perception and the Human Condition.

He also serves as a brand ambassador for The Times of India and contributes as a citizen journalist from Sydney.

Before migrating to Australia in 2000, Ruby spent over two decades with the Geological Survey of India. After settling in Sydney, he pursued various jobs, launched his own IT venture, and later expanded into real estate by founding his own business. Today, he is devoted full time to writing.

The Provocateur-Spilling Beans By All Means
Balvinder Ruby

All rights reserved
First Edition, 2022 (Hardcover) Coffee Table
Second Edition, 2023 (Hardcover) 6 x 9 inch
Third Edition 2025, (Paperback) 6 x 9 inch

No part of this publication may be reproduced, or stored in a retrieval system, or transmitted in any form by means of electronic, mechanical photocopying or otherwise without prior written permission from the author.

ISBN: 978-1-7614296-3-3
Genre: Poetry
Language: English
Dimensions: 6 x 9 inches

Disclaimer: The author and the publisher take no responsibility for any errors, emissions or contradictions that exist in the book.

TABLE OF CONTENTS

Introduction	7
You	8
Evolve	10
The Strategy	12
Pursuit	14
Hold Your Cards Close to Chest	16
Raise Your Bar	18
Open Letter to Myself	20
The Arrogance	22
The Chameleon	24
Hide and Seek	26
The Beauty	28
To Grow	30
Logical Emotions	32
I Love You	34

TABLE OF CONTENTS

Self Confidence	36
Cyborg	38
The Time	40
What Matters	42
Reality Check	44
COVID19	46
Manoeuvring	48
Bargain	50
Stay at Ease	52
Will Power	54
Probation	56
Without Any Doubt	58
The Curiosity	60
Appearance May Be Deceptive	62
The Trust	64

TABLE OF CONTENTS

Aspirations	66
With Malice Towards One and All	68
Brain Drain	70
An Illusion	72
Success	74
The Love	76
The Focus	78
Rattle the Kettle	80
Fashion	82

INTRODUCTION

This book intends to walk you through the length and breadth of your mindscape, arouse curiosity, invoke intellect and provoke you to reflect and realise your full potential so as to enable you to cruise the mundane daily grind harmoniously.

It seeks to dislodge you from your comfort zone, kick your butt, unsettle and prod you to start grappling for your mettle to get you thinking to the barge at large and take charge.

It is also directed to enrage you to engage and manage the stage, restrain to blame others, align you with your real true self and claim, seek and fight for your right without any insinuations and position you at the crossroads to decide for yourself whether and whither to here from and henceforth.

YOU

You may be wondering, who is this message for
Let me make it clear, it is for none other than you

Now don't ask what do I mean by you
Implying there are more than one you, in you

I warned you earlier to stay in one piece
It is not good to split yourself into two

Are you the one who is always on the run
To just have fun and enjoy the pun

Maybe you are the one who always shun
Public glare, limelight, shy and keep mum

Are you the one who always undermines yourself
Grumble stumble and don't see your worth

In that case, it is untrue and sure is a fallacy
Let's demolish decry and defy that prophecy

This message is of course for you if you care
It is for you if you have a moment to spare

This message is to ring the bell to tell
If you don't take charge, the hell

Is going to break loose with no option
To choose from, other than, to duck for cover

You may feel inclined this message sucks
Whatever you may think but this is the crux

EVOLVE

Move if you do not want to be tossed
Be on the move, grow and flow with time

Don't try to build physical or mental construct
However robust, it is bound to be demolished

Time is brute, better move and be astute
Don't stagnate and pollute, nothing is absolute

You can't afford just to be, a mute spectator
Evolve as the evolution demands

It reprimands those who resist and persist
Within no time they stop to exist

They get consigned and relegated as extinct
However oversized belligerent or extent

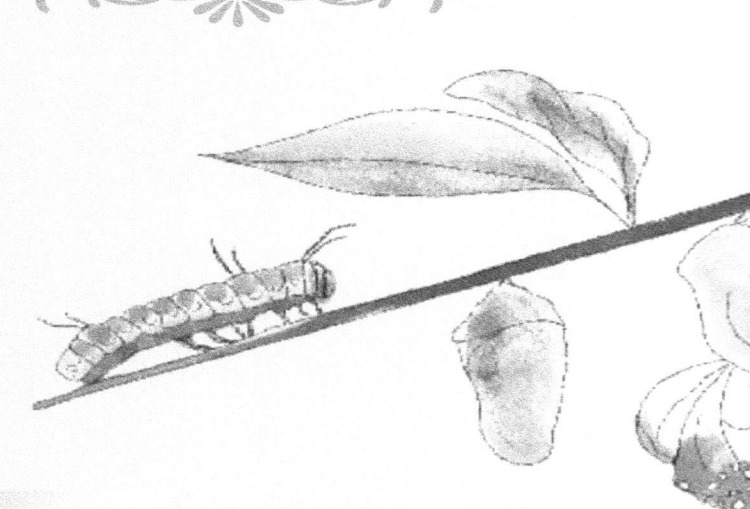

Foresee, embrace and lead the change
Evolve and flow imperceptibly with evolution

As it is bound to happen even if you do or don't
It bulldozes raizes and becomes a revolution

It amazes it rephrases it, it erases, it raises
Call it simply a change, evolution or revolution

You adopt it, resist it, fume it or subsume it
Flow with or grow with it or consume it

It is immaterial what you choose or refuse, to do
Whatever you do or whatever you arrange

It is bound to happen as it has always been
Happening and is bound to be called change.

THE STRATEGY

Make sure you are not understood easily
To avoid the risk of being branded a simpleton

Apparently, there is nothing wrong in appearing one
However, there is in fact an added advantage

As others will not feel insecure in your company
Would not deem it necessary to cross your path

As a result, leave you alone to operate unabated
As you don't interfere in their math.

That does not mean you have to be devious.
Even though advantages are obvious

Calling a spade a spade is fraught with danger and
As you run the risk of being labelled an uncouth

It is not a good idea to take the cudgel
Upon yourself to be the custodian of truth.

That does not mean you should allow
Yourself the luxury to be a sloth.

Don't be simply indolent either to avoid the trouble.
Take the courage to follow your convictions

That is probably the best course of action
To prove them wrong and their predictions

PURSUIT

Can you let me follow my pursuit
If that suits you or not is your purview

Perhaps I am a little or far off and
The time is not ripe and so is the context

As it must and it should be understood
Maybe I am taking a tree for the wood

It is not necessary for you to understand
My rhetoric just try to have a hang of it

I stand with you and I know that you know it
I will do whatever I can and deem it fit

To make sure you have a gut feeling and stay put
I am sure you will whatever be the rumour mill

There is a glaring gap that looks like a trap
You are and have to be the one to fill

I am out and about and ready to shout
At the top of my voice to make it clear

I am weary to wear the cloak of smoke
As you sure will be the one to stoke

I empower you and imbued you with the fire
To take cudgels irrespective of results being dire

HOLD YOUR CARDS CLOSE TO CHEST

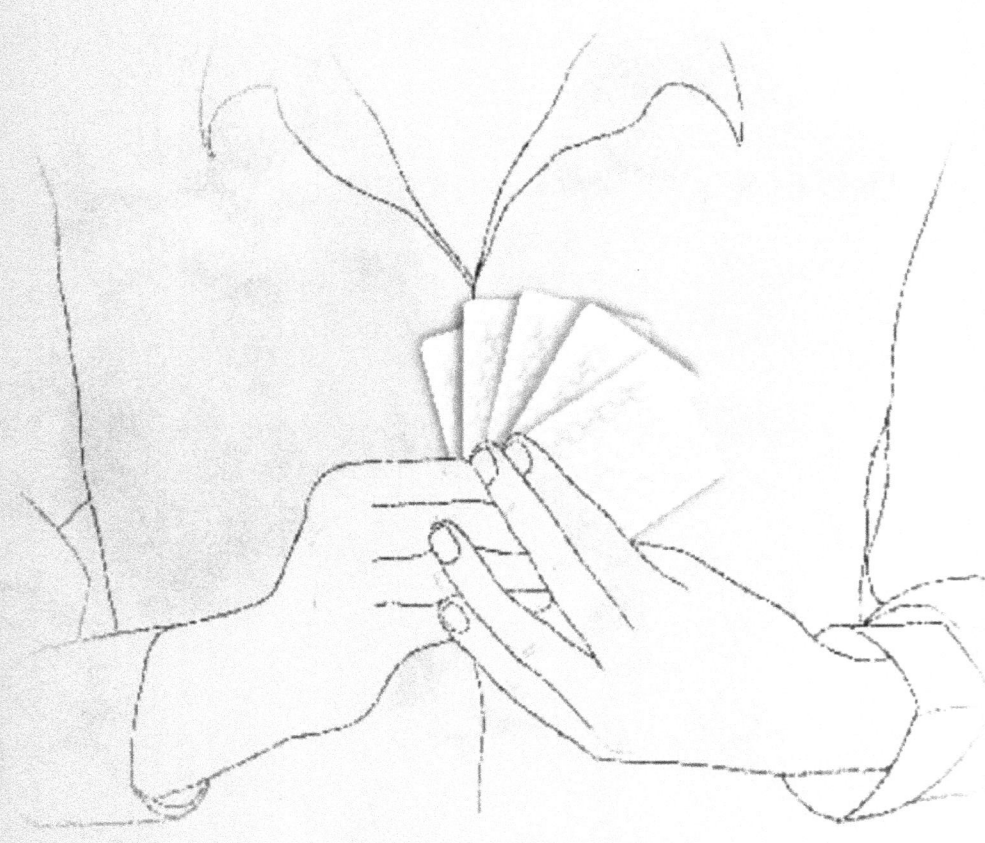

Who cares what is on your mind
What a ploy to suck you in their trap

They want to find from you what is on your mind
Then exploit your weakness and even strengths.

There are bloody sharks every step of the way out there.
It is their own interests if ever, they care

They are waiting for you to open your mouth and eat you alive.
Opening your mind is a far cry.

Be smart and let them bite the dust.
Don't ever floor yourself and bestow any sort of trust

Say everything and anything to avoid that you must.
Fool them around and keep your secrets to your chest at best.

Let your secrets be secret forever.
Keep them to yourself and be clever

In case you are suffering from an endemic of mind bloating.
Offload yourself to the clouds and let them be floating.

Don't forget to secure your cloud with a
PIN and to save your skin

RAISE YOUR BAR

Stand up, be counted, rise or even uprise
Don't bother to apprise, you don't need to
Avoid the pattern keep an element of surprise

Don't 'Will' run of the mill unless and until
You are doubly sure of the cure to endure
There is nothing as altar let the rumour mill

Keep grinding its finding and rewinding
Keep focus keep going and keep mowing doubts
About your potential and keep reminding

Even if you don't let me or give your permission
It makes no difference to me whatsoever
I will keep empowering you as per my mission

If you get stuck write it off as a bad dream
Refuel recharge get set to go at large
Enter the arena head-on with full steam

Let me tell you once you reach there
You wouldn't anymore care and it would not
Matter to you as your success wouldn't be rare

Once you reach there at the altar
You take it as normal and formal unknowingly and
Habitually keep raising your bar

OPEN LETTER TO MYSELF

I dare to write an open letter
Not to the power to be but myself

But why am I writing to a go-getter
Because, if not me, then who, I have no cue

Though you have and should have
A different view rather than rue

You have no right to expect anything
From anybody, if you are not putting your due

This is the only and the best way
To put to rest ifs, buts, whys and why not's

Thumping your chest is at best
Blowing your trumpet hollow

I don't know how you can digest it
When I can't even swallow

I have, no doubt, in your potential, though
You need to reset your priorities, my dear fellow

This letter can better be as relevant to
Yourself and elf anyone besides you who matters

Don't retract but protract and have the guts
Deflate and decimate the suckers and hard nuts

Stand up stand out and be counted not discounted
Don't merge or submerge or follow the currents

But make a difference with or without offence
In your defence though, with my few cents

THE ARROGANCE

If nothing is in white and blue,
Then what is the cue
When the truth is not absolute
Who do I solute

How do I blow my trumpet then
I don't know the flute
You may dump me as dumb
I prefer not to succumb

To your rhetoric
I prefer to be rather astute
I don't take that sort of fluke
As I am very resolute

You can't cow me down
You may think how cute
You may be numb to the
The sensuality of the common man

But you are mistaken to
Undermine my ilk and my clan
You are in fact histrionic
But definitely not the history

You are a clown and be frowned
Done dusted and drowned
You may try to wrap yourself
In a named pinstripe suit

Because you are shallow and hollow
My dear coward fellow
Soon you will be hooted out
Exposed, booed and rooted out.

I pity you rather and ask you to be wise
Approach a doctor, not a quack
Seek advice for split personality disorder
Before being pulled down and sacked

THE CHAMELEON

You think you can get away, sway
Manipulate and confound the public mood

How rude of you dude, wait for the day
For you, to decay, in public display and nude

There is a limit, to how far, the public will let you
Play with their sentiments so brazenly

Eventually will catch unaware and get you
You may tend to think the public does not know

Let me surmise you the public is letting you
Have a free play but will keep you on your toes

You think you are over smart old fart
But actually fast turning friends into foes

Raw sense only works on raw people but
You are dealing with people thick and dense

I know, you will take offence, and if you do
It indicates your shallowness, not prowess

You intend to get a place you don't belong
By obfuscating history you created a mess

Your actions are like a chameleon to keep
Changing appearance is not a mystery

Your compulsions, desperations, aspirations
Are definitely leading towards your decimation

HIDE AND SEEK

I tried my best to break free
Every time I tried I hit the breaks instead

I don't know and not sure if I love you
More I try to convince myself, I don't, but rue

Perhaps I do, but don't want you, to have a cue
I tried hard my feelings, to subdue

But that is perhaps, how it works in love
Love is nothing but a hide-and-seek game

Actually, I want somebody else, to deliver
The message, to you, to say the same

I found it a hard way, that it is actually, the case
As I lost control of my feelings to claim

Because it all depends on your whims or mood
If and when I am sad or happy or give a damn

THE BEAUTY

Beauty is in the eye of the beholder.
What would you like to be

A beauty, an eye or the beholder?
Beauty is what you perceive

It depends on and reflects your own mindset
Depending on what you have beset

The onus of responsibility squarely
Lies on you what you think beauty is

If you are honest you take others as one
If you are a crook you take others a spun

What you see in others is your own reflection
There are, though and of course exceptions

There is no dearth of psychopaths either
It is hard to identify them to get you wiser

There is a difference between being one
Maybe just posing but the harm is already done

Beauty is here there and all around
Just be on the look you will see it abound

It will surround and give you and uplift
Keep you afloat and frisk as that is its gist

TO GROW

I have an awfully bad habit of sermonising
Don't take me seriously

I will keep doing so, please
Don't take any offence

If you do, it is up to you
I have nothing to say in my defence

That could be my weakness
But I take it as credence

I will have a sleepless night tonight
To reflect on where I went adrift.

That is my story and that is the gist
I have put my case as simple and straight

Without enticing and without a bait
Without floundering, flabbergasting and taste

That is my throughout plan not put in haste
You are a liberated soul, not a copy and paste

Stay that way and need not say anything
That will be a sheer waste

Don't expect anybody even me to agree
With you, if you want to grow

LOGICAL EMOTIONS

It is logical to keep your logic at bay
If you can, do that and for how long

Depends on your strength
It is logical, to let it be that way.

It is logical to stay away
Let me pray that you get away

Hey, give way to emotions instead
Prevent the logic to let you sway

What an irony to using logic
To abandon the same, what a game

Give way to emotions and let them play
Have a field day I would like to say

Emote and let the logic decay
Because we are here to stay, come what may

I LOVE YOU

I don't have to prove it to anybody, not even you
That I love you, it does not matter whether
You are even aware, care or not or even realise
That, it is you, I mean you, and nobody else

That, I am referring to and pointing at
You, my pampered spoiled elusive
Dear darling, I miss, crave and yearn for
A part of my dream, scheme or beyond

Though I don't have to go around beating a drum
To keep shouting at the top of my voice
That I love you in fact and of course
Let me reiterate reinforce and be a bit hoarse

That I do so of course without any force
In essence with no offence to anybody
I love you for my own reasons or without one
Does not diminish in any way your relevance

I have no pretence and have nothing
In my defence, if you think otherwise to justify
Neither do I intend to clarify or say anything

In reference and hence neither do I pretend
As a result, I present here myself to be crucified
Denied, derided defied or as decided by you

SELF CONFIDENCE

Are you at peace with yourself?
If not be at ease, please
Feel released and be pleased with yourself
Don't shun your company

Let others have fun in your company
Smudge the grudge
Don't judge me as well yourself
Don't even fudge the facts and tacts

Play your role don't react
If you don't want others to direct you
What you should not and what you must
In yourself put all your trust

To avoid being washed adrift
Stay put, be your true self
Don't get carried away and swayed
Forlorn, torn and dismayed

I can only be with you and be your host
If you choose to be with yourself first and foremost

CYBORG

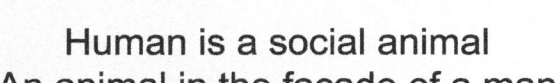

Human is a social animal
An animal in the façade of a man

In the absence of social constraints
It would behave like one

Driven by the basic instinct
Of survival of the fittest

You may call it might is right
The strongest and the bright

Might could be physical
Political social mental or financial

It could be in any form or shape
What matters is the differential

Biological evolution as propounded
By Darwin has now been grounded

For shifting the parameters
From biological and ecological

To intellectual as you may think
With the advent of artificial intelligence

Going to be supplanted and augmented with
It is taking us to a new level hereto and hence

By implanting a piece of technology
In the brain to speed up the processing

By then It will cease to remain human and
Transform itself I am confessing

Itself into a new being called Cyborg
A cybernetic organism that you may disdain

How will it work try to envision yourself
I have no idea or plan to explain

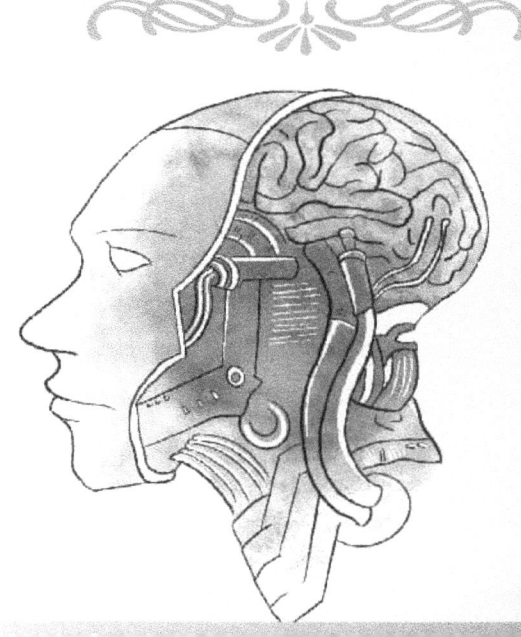

THE TIME

Have you noticed it gliding past?
It is a blank canvas and it is vast
If at all you need a hint

Depending on your instinct or stint
It is ephemeral and perennial
It is superficial but congenial
It creates ripples when pelted

It never stands still and hates to wait
It stretches as your imagination
It can also contract to date
Sometimes it looks as if standing still

It impregnates and relegates
Sometimes it gushes and rushes
You are amiss and it flushes
If you have still not realised

If you have not got it yet
What I am hinting at, it is fine
By the way, what I was referring to is
Nothing else but TIME.

WHAT MATTERS

It doesn't matter if you win or lose
It matters when you quit

It doesn't matter where you are going to
It matters when you are on the move

It does not matter what you do to make a living
It matters when you live to make a difference

It does not matter when you stand for yourself
It matters when you stand for downtrodden

It doesn't matter who you follow
It matters who follows you

It does not matter how fearful you are
It matters how fearless you are

It does not matter how powerful you are
It matters how you empower others

"Being the richest man in the cemetery doesn't matter to me. Going to bed at night saying we've done something wonderful...that's what matters to me."

Steve Jobs

REALITY CHECK

I don't have a dream but I have a scheme
Scheming? you may think, Not really

Because schemers stink of some sneaky mischief
Dreams act as a buffer zone for us to face reality

We like reality, do we, really? it is a myth
That we keep harbouring though

Evidently, it is a reality that
The myths do have a role to play

But what is not evident is that
There is no such thing as reality

Dreams are fascinating and we love to dream
Why so because they help us avoid reality

They take us on a virtual trip to skip reality and
Help us play a hide and seek game we loved as a child

As adults, we are neither interested in seeking nor hiding,
But in the game itself that gives us a thrill

The dreams, particularly the ones that we have
While awake, are like a hide and seek game

We dream actually to hide and then we start chasing
Our own self to find what we are hiding behind

We know where we are hiding and where to find ourselves
But we are having this exercise to have the thrill in the game

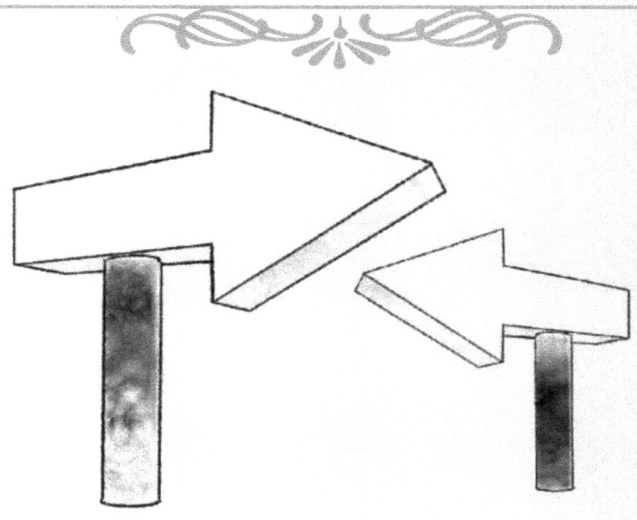

COVID 19

We are at the mercy of something that
Succumbs to soap but the thought of which
Makes us numb and our ego slump.

We kept looking for enemies left and right
For the traditional enemies but this one descended

From nowhere and took us by surprise
We kept building our nuclear and atomic arsenal

But the enemy turned out to be subatomic, subcellular.
This new enemy has brought home the point that

Our animosity is infructuous and grudges fissiparous
We are unnecessarily dissipating our energy and resources

On frivolous non-existent imaginary issues.
This new enemy has driven home this point to arch-rivals

To forget about their rivalry and pool up their resources and
Put up a joint front and stop playing the stunt

Of fooling their subjects just to keep their hold upon and
Mould their opinion to get them to agree and fall inline

This enemy will mark history and stand out
As a costly corrective for the human race from going berserk

MANOEUVRING

You are not supposed to know everything and
Not supposed to be in control all the times

What you are supposed is to understand that
The power dynamics do not stay the same

All the time and you have nobody to blame
Not even yourself elf you would like to lay claim

Know your strengths and weakness as well
It is the timing that matters I don't need to tell

It is not your strength only to dwell
It is opponents' miseries that need to swell

Understand the available options to win or
Play havoc for the opponent and create hell

It is a question of not only being decisive
But the timing to strike and quell

It is the timing of the strike that matter as no
The decision is absolutely wrong or right

It is the timing that matters
It is the decisiveness that rattles

Listen beam don't stifle
Play your cards be bright and sit tight

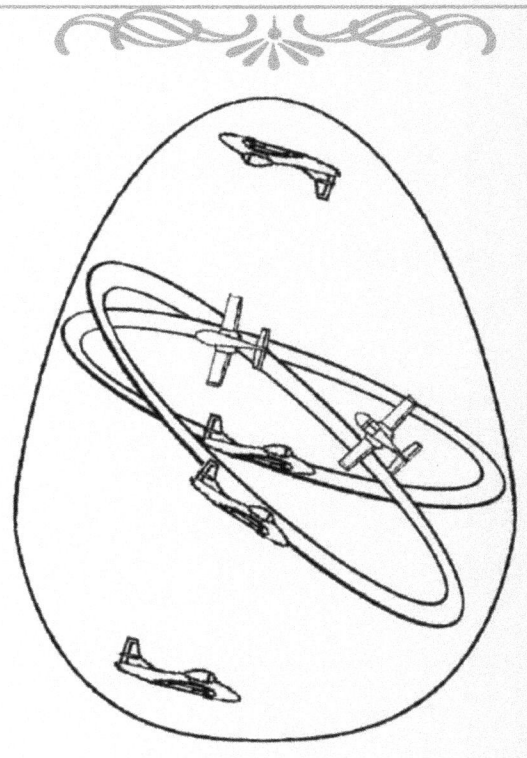

BARGAIN

Let me strike a bargain for you
By the way, why are you after the bargain

I can try just for your sake however
Let me tell you bargain is not worth the strain

I assure you my try will not accrue
What it entails as there is no gain without pain

Get up grow and throw your weight
Don't worry even if you overflow with disdain

My words fail me when I see people even
Superfluous with surplus don't refrain

It is time tested that the time invested
Is not the starter or appetiser but the mains

It is not a matter of priorities but getting
Them right otherwise all your effort just drains

It is not a question of fire fighting but
It is a question of who ignites it and who refrains

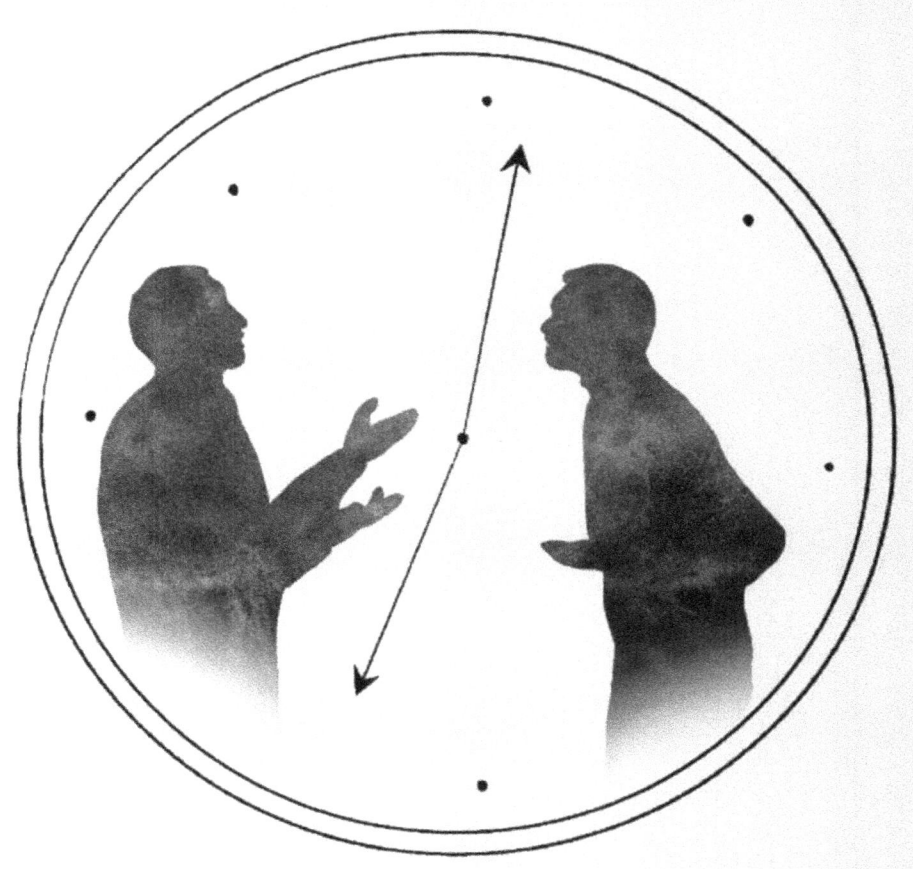

STAY AT EASE

The stark silence was characteristically
Noticeable by the absence of

The presence of reticence
Providing thereby a poignant moment

Perfect, pleasant and pertinent juncture
A blissful, blessed and concurrent

Thereby, essentially and differentially
Pregnating the environ with its essence

It is so wonderful a feeling for reeling
Why would anybody utter a word

Why would anybody say a thing?
In favour, for, against or in its defence

Why not nurture and culture a habit
Of not to look for ifs and buts and thence

Spend sleepless and restless nights
To look, seek and justify to get credence

Why would you tease and spew sleaze
When you can get there without all of these

It is a fallacy to believe that something
Is of no value if it comes by staying at ease.

Please yourself, please be and stay at ease

WILL POWER

Before exploring how to get there you
must know where you want to go.
Is it hard to understand if you are looking
for bread you need dow?

Going anywhere is no problem, the problem is
where you want me you to lead
You can go wherever you want,
provided it is not the greed

The proverb, where there is a will
there's a way stands true still
Whatever says the rumour mill it
still depends on your sheer will

It is straight and simple, there is no
trick no magic and no-frill
You don't need to be trained, you already
know it I don't need you to grill

The message is clear my dear without any
fear or empty spaces to fill
What you need to do is no dilly dallying
no frills but aim to kill

PROBATION

It is alright if you don't appreciate my love
But I do not appreciate you feeling unloved

Could it be you find a kick feeling that way or
You find a kick in giving that impression

Love is not finding and getting what you long for
But it lies in its pursuit and let it get away

Heer, Shashi, Laila, Ranjha, Punnu, Majnu
All the love sagas in history stand as a proof

Maybe you are the next one in the series
I am no special and can not afford to stay aloof

I will always be at pains to keep pains away
From you irrespective even if it ends as a goof

I am reeling under a sulking feeling
That is probably the part of the dealing

It is the journey, not the destination
It is where the pleasure is not it's a decimation

I believe in creating not following what is in fashion
However, I am not an expert but still on probation

I bow to the creator I am just the copycat
Not claiming copyrights just helping promotion

WITHOUT ANY DOUBT

There is a limit to what you can do
With your body, but there is no limit to
What you can do with your mind

I am sure I don't need to re-emphasize
This or remind you as it would not
Be hard for you to find

Don't get stuck in the frivolous grind
Raise your bar, step forward, stay ahead
Unafraid don't stay behind

Don't take anything granted, unwarranted and
Unwanted till you verify its veracity
Without applying your mind

Learn to discern the chaff from the grain
Train your mind to remain to stay in the frame and
Refrain from letting it drain in vain

Don't get contended unintended on starters
Rather keep a focus on the mains
If it's cloudy wait till it rains

It is worth reminding only if you mind and
Find it discerning and concerning
Grilling and thrilling with some gains

If it is not unsettling and rattling
It is not the worth and dearth of a kill
But still, it is worth a rumour mill

To fill the void and avoid the rot
It is a great ploy to employ to stamp out
The route and sprout instead a new thought

Without any doubt.

THE CURIOSITY

Keep your curiosity alive
To prevent the risk of dropping dead

It will feed your intellect, sharpen your
Acumen and the ability to reflect

Eat whatever you want to the extent of your intent
Don't worry to lose weight

If at all you feel the need to drop something
Drop the guilt, drop the ego, right

It has never been decided since the time
Immemorial what is true and what is right

It is not a matter of what and when
It is a matter of getting the priorities tight

If you come to pass and find the life stinking
Hunt for something to get you thinking

You would have no problem getting there
If you are able to rise above self

To get there you may need to shelve
Else try, dwell and delve

Into top gear to steer clear of the fear
Be rife to infuse veracity ferocity and of course curiosity

APPEARANCE MAY BE DECEPTIVE

The appearance may be deceptive
But not always, therefore, don't feel obliged
To whatever comes your way and be receptive

The apparently harmless may be invective
Stop believing the seemingly believable
Believe me, not even believe me never be restive

Whether you do or don't, believe me
Irrespective of your decision I am not going
To drop off my pretensions of being effective

I wouldn't stop prodding you to be incisive
Question not only me but your own self
Keep alive your inquest at best as a detective

Keep calm but build a storm in your mind
Do I need you to remind, that I stay behind
You to help you to be true to yourself or else

Somebody may take charge of yourself
Stoke provoke and use you before you even
Realise it is too late and you start to hate

Not only others around you even yourself
Be wary of such cunning elements
That looks very much your own to relate

THE TRUST

If you trust someone you bestow respect thereupon
It is natural, there is no jealousy no envy to frown down

The question, therefore, thus arises how to be trusted
If you try to bake it or fake it you will soon get busted

You need to have a sound footing and a solid base
Some sort of stubborn caress and a gleaming grace

Trust is highly regarded, has to be protected and guarded
If lost it can never be retrieved under any circumstances

If you don't care about being marauded, gutted or applauded
But stand by what you value you are the likely candidate

To be hated, smeared, berated but trusted
These values though intrinsic can, however, be inculcated

It is your insatiable desire and belly fire not to retire
But keep going, stowing, regrowing and de-weeding

If you follow something it starts receding
If you follow your passion it becomes a fashion

Don't follow let them swallow their pride
As a general guide, you have nothing to hide or deride

There is no hassle as you are not just an empty vessel
As you have been investing building trust not a castle

ASPIRATIONS

I have a dream
How does it matter if I do or don't

I am not Martin Luther King Jr
Still, I do have, not only one but many dreams

I even don't care if he holds any copyrights
To have dreams

I don't even care if his ghost comes alive and
Starts screaming at me how dare

You have a dream and
The guts to go online and onstream

It is fine to go online refine and define
It is not enough only to dream but

To rabble rouse everyone to follow suit
Because that is the only route

To conduit your passion and energies
To save yourself from the clergies

You are no less than RUBY, diamond or emerald
Go wild have a dream and surprise

WITH MALICE TOWARDS ONE AND ALL

I wish it was as simple as it seems
You may intend or tend to believe
The word conspiracy in that case would
Lose the meaning it has in its sleeve

You would say you don't understand
What it means probably is its context
I would wonder why is it so hard to understand
The simple statement at its best

To understand the grind and what is behind
It is utterly important to have an open mind
Having an open mind is to realise that
Everything has a context and nothing is defined

Don't rest on your credentials or your depth
Keep flowing and growing on the way
Don't forget mowing the insidious creepers
That try to entangle you and lead you astray

It is on purpose I am installing speed breakers
In your thought process to damper you
Otherwise, you will tend to surround yourself with
Self-seeker parasites that will pamper you

I am no sadist and derive no pleasure to rancour you
That is no highway but my way to empower you
I tend to be a circuit breaker issue raker risk taker
For your good and have no praise to shower on you

BRAIN DRAIN

When the governments of the day start sucking
Instead of caring for the people starts mucking

Intelligentsia feels suffocating and starts ducking
For the cover to recoup and recover the sap

Outside and away from the dysfunctional crap
Where what counts is intent and content not flap

When you try to refrain the brain to think and act
It will react and make a move to new and fertile ground

To you, it may sound profound and insane
Because you prefer them to decay and disdain

Who coined the term brain drain was perhaps lame
I feel sorry for him or her and it is a matter of shame

The brain always prefers to travel upstream like fish
There is no scope of going it down the drain going amiss

Population migration legal illegal or forced
Has led to the advancement of society, reinforced and

Endorsed the view that it is only few
Who protect you from getting screwed

It is the same lot you bracket as brain drain
It is only these people who are your saviours and protect

You to get framed as anti-national irrational
Who are not ready to rot get caught in the plot of the

Perverse criminal cunning liars who distort
Control and resort to anything above and beyond

Because they are sick and prick psychopaths
Insensitive and unaware of your forbearing and wrath

AN ILLUSION

What you think, who you are, is an illusion
If you think otherwise it would not be a surprise

To anyone or me because it is how it is supposed
To work, otherwise, everything will go berserk

It could be a matter of a rise or demise
Of the concept to enlist you as a suspect

Bereft or deft is beside the whole concept
It was creepy of someone to ask me if I am right or left

I don't position myself in their fossilised mental
Framework and framing everyone however obscene

It is too profound and beyond my dream
Let me take a chance to enhance your self-esteem

If you really and truly want to cherish and want to dream
Abandon the slumber and luxury of sleep

Be at ease with yourself don't worry about the crease
Try to keep awake don't ever let the sleep peep

It should not be a part of your design to resign
You don't even need a job of any APS level or benign

Keep yourself free as a tree to reach and access the sky
Don't sign on the dotted line and confine

To any person or systems design, give them a free hand
But tell them not to take you for granted and where you stand

SUCCESS

Before I ask if you think whether you consider
Yourself successful and find what do I refer

Let me clarify and until then defy, deride
To decide and keep your decision on hold and defer

Let me ask how you define what success means
Let's define actually what factually it seems

Does it mean having succeeded to get
What you were beset with and had a regret

Does success means to have achieved
Have got it and received or still feel deceived

Does success means to have reached
Wherever you wanted to or halted and breached

Does success mean to have learnt or earned
Health, wealth, happiness or you are not concerned

Did you mean by success, means, ends or journey
Success does not mean anything if you are mean

It has many meanings depending on your leanings
It too depends where you stand and what you pretend

It may have many or any meaning for a splintered
It is meaningless if you aren't in single piece and descent

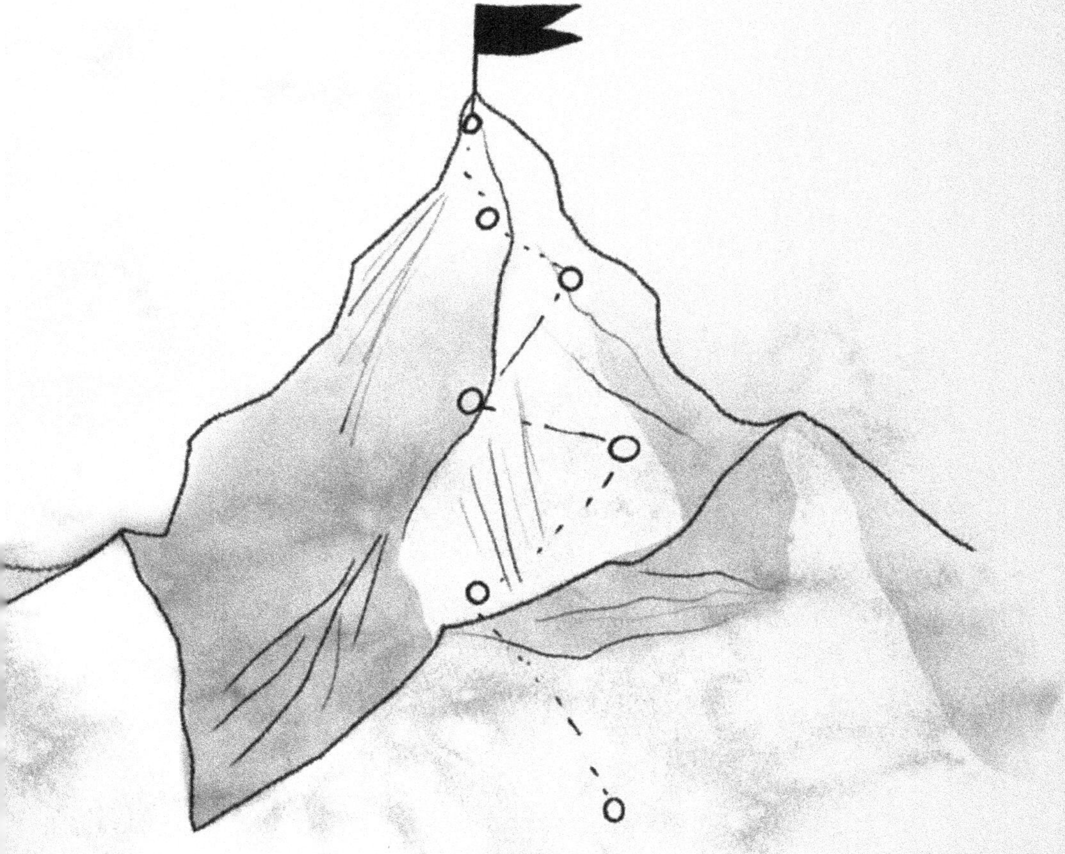

THE LOVE

I am love, pure simple below and above
So are you, this that him and her

Either you are not on the look to hook
With me, him her, are oblivious or don't prefer

To be a seeker but just presenting to be
That you are not and neither intend

But only pretend to hide behind yourself
Else your ego is not letting you bend

Trend, smother, and not let you bother
My sister, friend, contender or brother

It is easy to adjust and take to animosity
It is hard and scary to respond to being loved

Because it eliminates the element of fear
We have been ingrained and trained to rear

In our psyche since we abandoned the caves and
Overcome the mundane of thunder

Stopped to surrender to the natural raves
Have got accustomed to the imaginary splendour

Go out and find an abandoned lonely place
In the dead of the night where the time has no trace

Scream and yell at the top of your voice to rejoice
To find yourself in profound surround sound of choice

Engulfed all around with everything and anything
A ring of fire your eternal desire forever superb

The feeling, sensation, equation, relation, being
Belonging, longing, thronging treasure trove

I can't keep you guessing anymore a pure and simple
The eternal perennial elusive emotive sensation and feeling

That is called LOVE

THE FOCUS

Does it matter anyway who you are
What you do as long as you lift my spirits and
Help me to help somebody else
Including yourself for that matter

I have no reason to believe why you would
Not like me or anybody else to help you
As long as you are not a big ego and are in a position
To discount others as worthless as me.

Whoever you may be regardless, however
You can still help me to add an element that
Would be of some worth to somebody
To keep afloat seeking straw to hang on to

On average human uses only five per cent
Of its potential to achieve, attain or endeavour
To accomplish whatever he or she intends or
Wants to, what happens to the rest of ninety-five per cent

That remains underutilised and untapped and
Why is it not used, any guess?
It is not hard to find, the problem is not
The lack of potential in you

The problem is your potential not being
Put to use and remaining idle and untapped
The reason being it is not utilised is not the
Lack of your potential but the lack of your focus

As you are not able to grapple with any pertinent
Reason as to why you should do so, rightly and
Wrongly a reason not to do so
The question thus arises, despite you having

The underutilised potential are not able to use
It is because you do not have a reason to focus
It on to direct it at, have you ever wondered
Why the bloody hell you can not find any reason

To do something and focus your attention and
Energy upon and utilise your potential
To the fullest, the very reason is the lack of goal
I can assure you if you can define to do something

There is no power in the world that can
Stop you to attain, retain, regain and reframe the same

RATTLE THE KETTLE

It is easy to sail with a tailwind but your mettle
Is determined how and when you settle with a headwind

The life is not just to blow with the flow but rattle
The kettle and stand out not hackle but tackle

Show the way out, no doubt it unnerves
The nerd doesn't follow the herd if you have heard

It properly, keep yourself focused and coax yourself
To unclutter your mind of unnecessary grind

That keeps accumulating over time
If you are full to the brim, the important information

Which indeed is needed, will simply spill over unheeded
Therefore, it is important to declutter

Keep at least the reception area of your mind
Clean for the incoming traffic to be sent for grading

Before deciding what to do with it
It is where and when you need to recall your creativity

Creativity is your intrinsic attribute, a tribute
To you by the creator to another creator YOU to create

It does not have to be in a physical state I state, mate
Do not take refuge against fate, as you decide your fate

Don't wait, just take charge to forge ahead and
Make a difference and leave behind your footsteps

For posterity, though it may have no meaning
The meaning makes no sense, in essence, and hence

Do not route distraught in the thought to seek meaning
In whatever you do but find pleasure in your quest to seek

Don't feel meek but stand still and quiet to realise
Your might learning is a lifetime exercise

Said my friend who is a sage, which is not a surprise
You will advise but strut and stumble if you are not humble

Yearn to unlearn should be your concern
Instead, I am afraid to say that being the way

To be innocent like a newborn to adorn and appreciate
The form, and mourn the death of knowledge and acknowledge

You know nothing and don't even bother to know the known or
Anyone who wants to be known let the known

Be enthroned to the dust of times to come that cares
Not at all to install the fallen or the ones who align

With the powers of the day who think they will stay
Nay, come what it may.

FASHION

Don't hide but take pride in being one staying true
Believe in creating not following what is in fashion

Fashion is for the followers, bring out the leader in you
Followers and leaders are a different creed indeed

Followers and fans are meant to feed the need
Swell the ego of hollow and shallow breed

Leaders are beyond and always around when you need
They don't suck and muck around but empower and lead

It doesn't matter what you wear or smear your wear
Steer clear of your line of thinking without blinking

Your veneer, your cladding is prone to weathering
Your kernel is where resides your eternal journal

Don't be shrouded and get your vision clouded
Don't even worry about being marauded

Be and behove the treasure trove of splendour
A guiding star enormous enigmatic open and ajar

An epicentre a hope a chance to enhance
To enfranchise endorse and enforce perforce

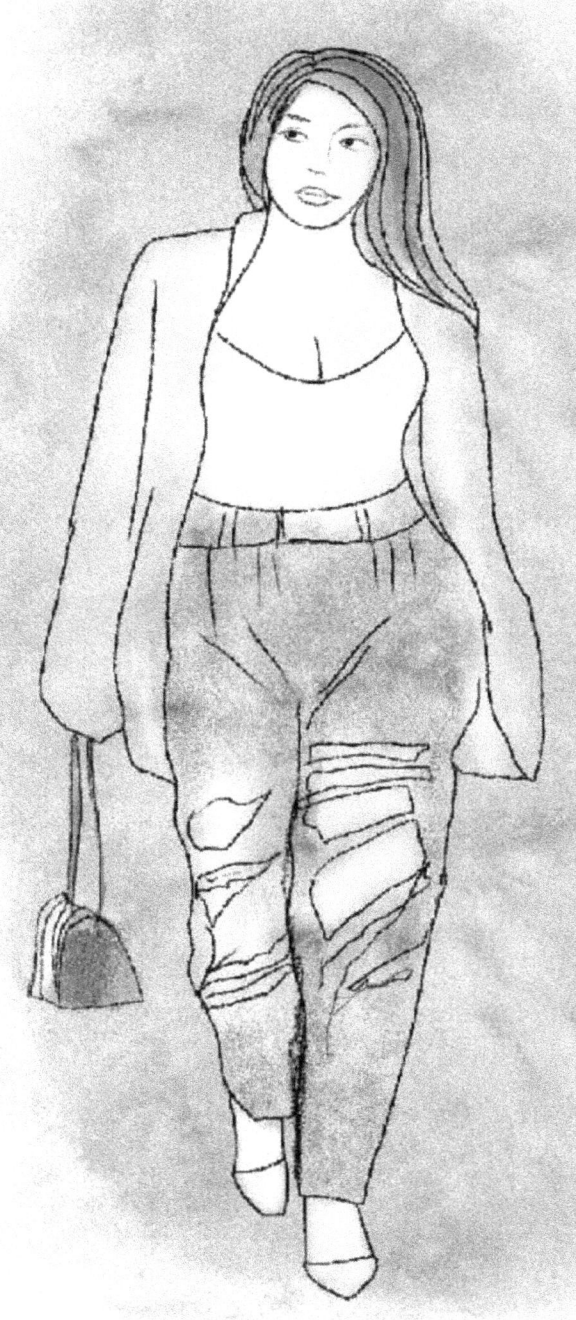

www.ingramcontent.com/pod-product-compliance
Lightning Source LLC
Chambersburg PA
CBHW040638100526
44583CB00039B/3204